SUCCESS UNTANGLED

30 Life Lessons That Lead to Achievement

JENNIFER MARTIN

This book has been published with the intention of providing helpful and informative content. The publisher and the author make no representations or warranties of any kind with regard to the completeness or accuracy of the contents of this book and specifically disclaim any implied warranties of

merchantability or fitness for any
particular purpose. The advice and
strategies contained herein may not be
suitable for every situation.

Table of Contents

Introduction

"At the end of the day, an individual's level of success is what counts."

—Tina Miller

This book is the definitive guide to leading a prosperous life. Success in life is not difficult, despite what you might think. You can take the actions required to realise all of your aspirations and goals if you have the proper perspective, attitude, and information.

This book promises to help you discover the key to success. It is brimming with significant, applicable life lessons that will aid in your full potential realisation. You will discover the fundamentals needed to succeed in both your personal and professional lives and reach any goals you have set for yourself.

It includes a compilation of tips from successful thinkers, businesspeople, and influencers in addition to explaining the principles of becoming successful. Every single one of these tales contains a life lesson that will help you succeed. We aim to demonstrate to you that success is attainable with perseverance and hard work.

We'll go into more detail on the value of having an action plan, how to thrive in trying circumstances, and how to refine your success criteria.

Most importantly, this book will teach you how to maintain motivation and keep your attention on what matters. We will also go into the methods you should use to continually work towards your objectives in order to have long-lasting benefits.

In the end, the goal of this book is to direct you towards success by assisting you in making thoughtful judgements. We wish you a pleasant voyage and the realization of your full potential.

Set attainable and realistic objectives.

"Tie your happiness to a goal, not to people or things, if you want to live a happy life."

One of the most crucial things a person can do to succeed in life is to set attainable and realistic goals. It gives you direction and clarity, allowing you to concentrate your efforts and gauge your success. We are better equipped to assess our successes and failures and modify our strategy when we have defined targets.

It's crucial to make sure your goals are both attainable and reasonable when you set them. Unrealistic expectations could lead to failure and discouragement. Goals that are too simple could not be enough to motivate you and won't successfully encourage you to work harder and develop. Be realistic about what you can do by taking into account your abilities, expertise, and experience at this point.

Clearly defined objectives should also be used. Outline the actions you'll take to get where you're going in the end. Determine the resources, equipment, and potential difficulties you'll need to overcome them. Your journey can be divided into manageable phases, which will help you move forward and stay on course.

Goals that were once attainable may no longer be so as time goes on because of the ongoing change in our life. Keep an eye on your objectives and revise them as necessary. Modify an existing objective or create a new one if you feel it to be overly challenging or irrelevant.

We may make our aspirations come true by setting goals that are both attainable and reasonable. You'll be more likely to stay on track, stay inspired, and eventually accomplish your goals if you have structure, direction, and purpose. Never lose concentration, put in extra effort, or quit up. Anything is attainable with effort, time, and dedication.

Create a solid work ethic.

"I worked hard and never feared my abilities."
—Michael Jordan

Success depends on having a good work ethic because it shows commitment, tenacity, and general attitude towards one's job. An individual's willingness to work hard and accept responsibility for their actions is reflected in their work ethic, and this will ultimately lead to their productivity and success.

Strong work ethic possessors frequently exhibit a positive attitude and a proactive approach. They realise that in order to succeed, they must put in a lot of effort and work long hours. These people are self-disciplined and set boundaries and priorities for their workday. They typically concentrate on the most important things and may remain committed to their work despite challenges. As a result, the work produced is of greater quality. Additionally, these people are considerably more capable of overcoming difficulties.

Personal and professional development are supported by a strong work ethic. Individuals' productivity rises and success occurs as they concentrate on being the best versions of themselves. Working hard increases a person's chances of achieving their objectives and improving everyday performance. A strong work ethic also results in greater pride and satisfaction in one's accomplishments, which inspires one to persevere.

Adopting a strong work ethic is also advantageous for job advancement. High-commitment employees are able to advance in responsibilities and receive greater praise from their bosses. People who can work hard and produce results are willing to be hired by businesses.

Success in life requires a strong work ethic. It fosters growth on both a personal and professional level, increases accountability, and aids people in achieving their life objectives. Strong work ethic allows individuals to perform better every day and receive more praise from their employers. Furthermore, those who exhibit dependability and accountability are more likely to be picked for positions with greater responsibility. Ultimately, a person's devotion, tenacity, and general success-oriented outlook are reflected in their work ethic.

Clarify your goal.

"Once you clarify your purpose for doing something, the way to do it becomes clear."

—Oprah Winfrey

One of the most important things you can do to achieve success in life is to identify your purpose. Clarifying your purpose may be a powerful and instructive exercise that serves to guide every decision and action you take. This will assist you in staying on track and keeping your focus where it needs to be.

Having a clear sense of purpose allows you to set meaningful and attainable goals. It provides you something to aim for and the incentive to keep working hard and pushing yourself to achieve your objectives. Clarifying your purpose creates a feeling of direction that allows you to stay focused on what you want to do, regardless of the obstacles that may arise. It also keeps you motivated and reminds you why you work so hard.

Having a goal helps you stay motivated and disciplined. When you have a goal in mind, it can be simpler to make the sacrifices and changes in your life that are required to achieve it. Knowing your mission and being focused on what you want to achieve will provide the discipline needed to stay on course.

Setting defined goals also aids in directing your efforts to ensure that they will assist you in achieving your intended outcome. This assists you in identifying the actions you will need to follow and prioritising tasks so you can stay focused and complete them. This also helps you to delegate work that you are not as good at, allowing you to better manage your time and focus on the duties that you are strong at.

Finally, having a strong sense of purpose can help you stay motivated and inspired. It will give you the drive and passion to keep trying even when things get tough. It will also keep you focused on your principles and views, ensuring that you are doing something that benefits both you and others.

To summarize, understanding your purpose is a great method to achieve success in life. It aids in providing direction and inspiration; setting significant goals; and keeping you focused, disciplined, and motivated. All of these factors work together to help you make your aspirations a reality and achieve the level of success you seek.

Surround yourself with successful, positive people.

"Surround yourself with people who will lift you higher."

—Oprah Winfrey

Developing nice and successful relationships in your social circles is an excellent strategy to achieve success in life. When you socialize with people who are ambitious, driven, and motivated, your subconscious mind receives a powerful message that you, too, want to be successful. This, in turn, can increase your ambition and motivation, as well as help you develop a better work ethic.

It is critical to associate with people who respect hard effort and have a positive attitude on life. When you surround yourself with successful individuals, it can help you create goals and push yourself to new levels of achievement. It can be difficult to achieve your goals if you are surrounded by people who do not commit and give up easy.

Successful people are often humble and willing to mentor and offer their knowledge and advise. This can be really beneficial in moving you closer to your objectives. When someone has achieved success in an area you are attempting to pursue, they can provide useful advice, suggestions, and techniques to assist you progress in your own success journey. Networking and developing relationships with positive and successful people can also lead to opportunities that you would not have had otherwise.

Furthermore, people with a proven track record of achievement frequently exhibit good behaviours that you can imitate and emulate. Successful people, for example, typically have excellent time management skills, the ability to prioritise activities, and an eye for detail. They are also excellent planners and understand how to manage their time well. As a result, you can observe and learn various ideas and techniques for increasing your productivity.

Successful people are aggressive and energetic, and they inspire those around them. When you are surrounded by people who are continually looking for solutions and do not give up easily, it frequently stimulates you to aim higher and act more confidently in order to achieve your goals. It can also be beneficial to be surrounded by supportive people who offer constructive criticism and comments to help you improve and grow.

Finally, surrounding oneself with good and successful individuals might help you achieve success in life. As an individual blends into their environment, absorbing the personalities and energy of the people in the group, associating with successful and driven people can help them achieve success more easily and rapidly.

Develop self-control.

"Discipline means choosing between what you want right now and what you want most."
—Abraham Lincoln

Self-discipline is a crucial aspect in determining one's level of success in life. Self-discipline can help an individual achieve their goals, stay organized, and lay a solid basis for their future.

To begin with, self-discipline assists an individual in remaining motivated and driven to achieve their goals. Having the self-discipline to stay focused and committed to the task at hand can make all the difference in attaining success, whether in an academic context or in the workplace. For example, having the discipline to set aside time to thoroughly prepare for a test can mean the difference between passing and failing. Similarly, having the self-discipline to put in the extra effort and take on challenging duties in the office will assist ensure that the individual is perceived as reliable and capable of taking on more important roles.

Developing self-discipline also contributes to the formation of a clear and organised attitude. Having the motivation and resolve to stay structured and on target helps save a person from feeling overwhelmed and unable to accomplish their responsibilities on time. Procrastination can frequently result in missed deadlines and unmet commitments, but having the self-discipline to be organised can assist an individual in staying on target and ahead of schedule. For example, having the self-discipline to develop a daily calendar and split things down into small portions might help you stay focused and accomplish chores efficiently.

Finally, self-discipline can assist an individual in laying a solid basis for their future. An individual can create a good reputation and become a valuable member of any team by being able to stick to a schedule, stay organised, and take on difficult jobs. An employer, for example, is more inclined to hire and promote someone who has demonstrated discipline and commitment to success. Furthermore, being self-disciplined enough to stay on track and put in the extra effort might lead to better prospects and job progression.

To summarise, self-discipline is vital for obtaining life success. It assists an individual in being motivated, structured, and focused while also laying a solid basis for their future. Anyone can develop the qualities and skills required for success with a strong commitment to self-discipline.

Learn from your errors.

"Anyone who has never made a mistake, has never tried anything new."

—Albert Einstein

Learning from mistakes is an essential aspect of achieving success in life. Mistakes teach us vital lessons that can help us improve our skills, problem-solving techniques, and make better, more informed judgements in the future.

Resilience is one of the most significant lessons to be gained from mistakes. Everyone will face losses in life, but the capacity to get back up and keep going is essential for success. From minor missteps to major dangers, the more we cultivate this mindset, the more adaptable we become in life.

Another essential skill learned through failures is risk analysis. When something doesn't go as planned, it's critical to assess what went wrong, what could have been done better, and how to avoid making the same mistake again. We are more prone to repeat our mistakes if we do not learn from them. The more mistakes we make, the more we can learn to analyse and evaluate a scenario in order to reduce risk and make an informed decision.

Rather of becoming discouraged by failures, it is critical to approach learning with an open mind. Understanding what we don't know and how to get the knowledge we need to move forward requires becoming more conscious of our limitations. Education is a life-long process, and we only take the time to become informed and learn what we missed when we face significant circumstances.

Finally, mistakes can teach us humility and compassion. When we can relate to someone on a personal level, we are more inclined to feel empathy for them, and making errors can be a terrific approach to find common ground. Our shared experiences enable us to become closer and more understanding of one another.

Mistakes can help us become more successful in life by teaching us essential lessons ranging from developing resilience to appreciating the value of risk analysis, education, and compassion. With a learning-focused growth mindset, we can turn mistakes into successes and use our experiences to gain confidence in our decision-making abilities.

Persevere in the face of hardship.

"The only way to guarantee failure is to stop trying."

—Tina Miller

Perseverance in the face of hardship is a necessary attribute for life success. Adversity is not limited to a single event; it can manifest itself in a variety of ways. It could be working conditions, a painful sickness or injury, incorrect assumptions, financial issues, personal relationships, or even failure. To achieve our objectives and be successful, we must cultivate the resilience and mindset required to persevere in the face of adversity.

Although it may appear to be a difficult endeavour, overcoming hardship is possible. There are several key approaches to accomplish this. The first and most crucial thing to remember is to stay focused on the eventual objective. When confronted with a challenging situation, it is normal to become overwhelmed and lose sight of what is important. Remind yourself frequently of why you are fighting and what you hope to achieve. Consider what is at stake and why you are experiencing such difficulty in the first place.

The second important factor is to rely on your support network. It is critical to have people near to you on whom you can rely. Having someone who can provide you guidance and support during difficult times can help you stay on course and make it through. It is also critical to reflect on your accomplishments and what you have already overcome.

Consider the following scenario: you are applying for employment but have been continually denied. It is critical to remain positive in this scenario and see it as an opportunity to progress rather than a severe setback. Remind yourself of the difficulties you have previously overcome and what you have accomplished.

It is also critical to never quit. Even when it appears that all hope is lost, keep looking for solutions and alternate routes. Use the resources at your disposal and keep striving. Although it may appear hard at times, the most successful people experienced many problems that appeared insurmountable but were able to continue.

Finally, remember that perseverance is a process, and while it might be difficult and challenging, achievement is achievable. Perseverance will be rewarded.

Perseverance Examples:
- Steve Jobs was sacked from Apple in 1985, but went on to found Pixar, a breakthrough animation firm, before returning to Apple.
- After battling addiction and despair for a long time, Grammy-winner and actress Lady Gaga eventually achieved success in her music career and is now an activist for mental health awareness.
- John Maclean, who was paralyzed from the waist down in a skiing accident, became the first paraplegic to complete the Ironman Triathlon.

- Oprah Winfrey built a globally famous talk show, media production company, and magazine despite dropping out of high school.

Finally, it is through the difficulties we have encountered that we have gained the strength and bravery to succeed. Perseverance is the quality required to face these seemingly insurmountable challenges and learn from them in order to improve and progress. This trait can be developed to help you get through any scenario, attain success, and achieve your goals.

Take chances.

"Living with equipment prevents us from taking risks, and if you don't go out on the branch, you'll never get the best fruit."

—Sarah Parish

Taking chances might be a necessary step towards success in life. Taking chances entails stepping outside of your comfort zone and forcing yourself to do something you are not familiar with. It can be a challenging step, but it can open many doors and help you achieve your goals in life.

Let's start with the definition of risk. The Cambridge Dictionary defines risk as "the possibility of something bad happening" or "the possibility that you may be harmed or lose something of value." It sounds terrifying, but it doesn't have to be. Everyone is terrified of something, but it should not prevent you from reaching your objectives. Taking chances can help you grow and develop as a person. It might assist you in breaking free from old routines and pushing yourself to go further and do more.

Applying for a job that appears to be outside of your skill set is one example of taking a risk in order to succeed in life. You could be scared, but if you don't apply, you'll never know what might have occurred. Even if you lack all of the qualifications required for the job, it is critical to believe in yourself. Take a chance and apply. The outcome may surprise you.

Starting your own business is another example of taking a risk in order to achieve success in life. It's a risk because you'll be investing a lot of your own time and money, but it may also be incredibly profitable. Taking a risk can be difficult, but it can offer up a world of opportunities.

Finally, taking chances can help you become more creative. If you're working on a project, take a chance and try something unconventional. You might be surprised by the outcomes. Taking chances allows you to experiment with new ideas and push yourself further than you have previously.

Finally, when it comes to achieving success in life, taking chances can be incredibly advantageous. It allows you to step outside of your comfort zone and challenge yourself, which can lead to rewards and progress in the long run. Taking risks might be scary, but if you stay brave and dedicated, you can achieve incredible things.

Stay Focused.

"Remain focused, pursue your dreams, and keep moving forward."

—LL Cool J

One of the most fundamental factors for success in life is the ability to focus. The ability to focus on a job or objective is essential for obtaining outcomes and increasing productivity. A person who can keep their attention on a single aim will have better clarity and a more positive attitude. This mindset can lead to wiser decisions and a more prosperous existence.

Improved concentration is one advantage of keeping focused. When you concentrate on a single task, you block out all other distractions and devote your entire mental energy to that work. This increased concentration aids in both the quality and speed with which you do your assignment. Concentration increases your ability to think clearly and pay attention to the specifics of the activity, allowing you to think analytically and come up with superior answers.

Second, staying concentrated aids in stress reduction. It might be tough to keep track of what has to be done when you have many tasks to complete at the same time. This might lead to feelings of overwhelm and stress. Focusing on one activity at a time, on the other hand, makes it easier to keep on top of what needs to be done. This not only saves you time, but it also relieves stress.

Finally, maintaining attention can lead to increased production. When you concentrate on a single activity, you may optimise your efforts and devote all of your energy to that one aim. This boosts your productivity by allowing you to perform things more quickly and effectively. Furthermore, by making modest, attainable goals and focusing solely on those chores, you increase your chances of being motivated and effective. In the long run, this can lead to better results.

Let's imagine you're attempting to create a book. It can be difficult to make progress if you try to do too many things at once, such as writing, researching, and editing. Instead, devote a set amount of time to one endeavour, such as writing. This will help you stay focused and complete your goal of writing the book.

To summarize, keeping focused is a crucial ability for achieving life success. It improves concentration, reduces stress, and boosts productivity. In order to be effective, it is critical to practice and increase your capacity to focus on a particular job or objective.

Take advice from successful individuals.

Learning from successful people is an excellent strategy to achieve success in life. We can learn a lot about what it takes to succeed by studying the pathways of individuals who have already succeeded. There are numerous examples of people who achieved success by learning from those who came before them.

For example, Facebook creator Mark Zuckerberg was highly influenced by Steve Jobs and his attitude to business. He learned from him that having a quality product and taking advantage of as many possibilities as possible is the key to success. As a result, Zuckerberg was able to transform his Facebook idea into one of the world's largest and most successful corporations.

Elon Musk, the founder of Tesla and SpaceX, is another example. Musk was inspired by people like Thomas Edison and Nikola Tesla, who demonstrated that success could be achieved via innovative thinking and a never-ending desire to improve things. Musk also drew on lessons from other successful entrepreneurs, such Jeff Bezos and Peter Thiel, to construct his own success techniques.

The lesson here is that in order to be successful in life, it is necessary to learn from those who have already succeeded. We can learn a lot about what it takes to be successful by examining their methods. We can also acquire valuable lessons about how to deal with adversity, stay motivated, and create strong support networks.

Finally, keep in mind that learning from successful individuals is not a one-way route. While we can undoubtedly draw inspiration from others, we must eventually build our own ways of thinking and methods to achievements. In the end, the combination of what we learn from others and the unique techniques we develop on our own will determine our success.

Network efficiently

Networking is an essential component of life success because it provides access to resources, people, and opportunities that would otherwise be unavailable to an individual. Networking can open doors in a variety of fields, including professional, business, educational, and social. A strong network of contacts may help you build a successful career, uncover new business prospects, and even locate mentors and sponsors to help you progress in many areas.

Professional networking is essential for success. Effective networking can assist in the development of relationships and trust with potential employers or employees. Developing relationships with one's coworkers can lead to enhanced prospects for advancement, access to essential contacts and information, and personal recognition. In the long run, networking can assist a person in finding more important and effective employment inside a business.

On a professional level, networking can assist entrepreneurs in gaining access to the tools and contacts they require to expand their enterprises. It's critical to establish a strong personal network of like-minded experts who can offer guidance when things get tough. Participating in local networking events and clubs can help one discover local resources and contacts that can be essential in establishing one's business. Furthermore, networking is critical in developing strategic alliances and collaborations to obtain access to resources and knowledge to assist a business in reaching its objectives.

Networking is vital in education for gaining credentials and improving educational knowledge. It is critical to establish relationships with instructors and other students in order to receive guidance or obtain access to research possibilities. Furthermore, networking with industry leaders and alumni can help you build technical skills, evaluate career options, and apply for internships and fellowships.

Finally, networking can be beneficial in the social world. Creating social connections is essential for building relationships and discovering one's interests. Attend social events and join groups or clubs relevant to issues of interest in order to meet new people and locate people who share your interests and values.

Overall, effective networking is a critical component of success in many fields. It is beneficial when looking for new chances, making connections, and forming long-term relationships that can lead to good outcomes. By developing meaningful contacts, it is possible to grow resources and knowledge, finally resulting in the creation of an exceptional network.

Make a plan and stick to it.

Making and sticking to a plan is an important part of achieving success in life. People who have attained their life goals have made plans and worked hard to follow them. A focused effort and dedication are required to achieve goals. A person cannot be successful in life unless they have a plan for getting there.

Setting realistic and achievable goals is one of the most critical components of designing a plan. People who have found success in life know what they want and how to attain it. They determine the steps necessary to make their goals a reality. Successful entrepreneurs, for example, frequently establish a business plan that defines the steps that must be performed in order to launch the business and accomplish the intended goals. Setting short-term and long-term goals provides them with a road map to follow.

Furthermore, successful people plan ahead of time and keep to it. They ensure that the necessary measures towards their goals are taken in a timely manner. This keeps them on track and prevents them from becoming distracted by other projects or hobbies. A successful artist, for example, may construct a timeline outlining when they will finish their artwork, practise their trade, and interact with other professionals in the art industry. They ensure that their efforts will be rewarded by adhering to a timetable.

Successful people must also be adaptable and modify their plans as needed. They recognise that plans might alter and that new possibilities and challenges may arise. Being adaptable and open-minded allows people to seize chances and make the required modifications to adapt to new situations. A successful athlete will be able to modify their training regimen to suit injuries or changes in the competition scene.

Making a plan and sticking to it are critical for success. People who have realized their aspirations recognise the value of setting realistic goals, keeping a timeframe, remaining adaptable, and remaining inspired. They devise a strategy and stick to it in order to attain their objectives.

Set yourself deadlines.

Setting a personal deadline, for example, might assist guarantee that you stay on track and cover the essential content in time for the exam if you are studying for an impending test. With this deadline, you will be reminded of when the test is, what needs to be studied, and how far you need to go. This will help you stay focused and motivated during your study session.

Setting deadlines for oneself is a critical component of achieving life success. Deadlines help you stay motivated, focused, and dedicated to attaining your objectives and dreams. They give structure and encourage accountability, preventing activities from being procrastinated or otherwise neglected. Having deadlines for other activities in life that must be fulfilled is just as vital. Deadlines help you stay organized and ensure you don't neglect anything vital. Life can become rather chaotic without them. For example, if you're attempting to complete a major project at work, divide it into smaller, achievable projects and attach personal deadlines to each of them. This will help you stay organized because each individual task will have its own aim and deadline.

Deadlines can also help encourage you. Knowing that you must accomplish a task in x amount of time will motivate you to work diligently and intensively to complete the assignment swiftly and efficiently. This sense of urgency will also provide you with a sense of accomplishment once the activity is accomplished, since you will have completed it before the deadline. For example, if you are working on a long project, you should set sub-deadlines for each step of the project. This will provide an incentive to continue working and make timely progress on the project.

Finally, deadlines can be a great instrument in assisting you to attain success. It enables you to stay organised, focused, and motivated in order to complete activities on time and with minimal effort. It also gives you a sense of achievement when you complete a task, ensuring that you are consistently making progress towards your goals.

Set priorities for your tasks.

Prioritizing your duties enables you to focus on the most important activities first, allowing you to achieve progress in the areas that truly matter. It is a technique that enables you to prioritize your duties, resulting in improved work performance and increased effectiveness and efficiency in reaching goals. For example, if you work in an organization and your job demands you to handle multiple activities in a day, it is critical that you prioritize those duties so that you may finish them as efficiently as possible.

Prioritizing your duties might help you become more structured and develop better plans. Knowing which jobs are the most important and which must be accomplished first will help you schedule your day correctly. Once you know what has to be done, you can quickly prioritize those jobs to maximize your time and resources. For example, if there are critical deadlines, you can designate additional time to accomplish the projects and prioritise them, while other jobs that can wait can be scheduled later.

Furthermore, prioritizing your duties might boost productivity by allowing you to focus and stay motivated. Because it is easy to become overwhelmed by a large number of duties, having a priority list ensures that you prioritize the most critical things first. Concentrating on one activity at a time helps you to devote all of your attention to finishing it and moving on to the next. It might help you stay motivated by reminding you of the progress you've made towards your goal.

To summarize, prioritizing your chores is a terrific approach to ensure success and should be used to become more organized, productive, and capable of meeting goals. It assists you in determining which tasks are most important and prioritizing them in order to maximize your time and resources. It can also help you stay motivated because you can see your progress and the goals you've met, giving you a sense of success and pride.

Make use of technology.

Technology has become an inseparable part of our lives, and it can be a tremendous instrument for achieving success. Using technology efficiently can help us interact with others, manage our duties, keep organized, and research information. Connecting with other people is one way that technology might help us become more successful in life. Maintaining personal and corporate connections requires effective communication. Email, texting, and video conferencing, among other technologies, can offer effective and timely contact with people who would otherwise be impossible to communicate with owing to distance and other hurdles. Furthermore, social media platforms such as Facebook and Twitter can assist individuals in sharing their achievements with a large audience. This can assist, boost confidence and foster relationships with others.

Another way that technology can assist us in becoming more successful in life is in managing day-to-day tasks. Technology can assist us in being organized by giving apps that remind us of future tasks and deadlines. Technology can also help to automate mundane tasks such as tracking fitness objectives with wearable devices and creating an event calendar. We can reduce the amount of time it takes to complete tasks by managing them efficiently, as well as confusion and tension.

Staying organized is critical for success, and technology may help with this. Online filing systems, such as Dropbox, enable us to save and access documents and files in the cloud. There are other apps that can help us organize our daily activities, such as taking notes and generating lists. Having a system in place to keep track of our responsibilities, schedules, and information can free up our mental bandwidth, allowing us to focus our time and attention on more important concerns.

Finally, technology can help us succeed in life by giving us access to research and knowledge. The internet and search engines are powerful tools that can help us gain access to the knowledge we need to flourish in our chosen career. There are other data collection services that can supply us with up-to-date industry trends and competition information. Having access to the knowledge we need for our field can help us stay ahead of the game and compete effectively.

To summarize, technology can be a powerful instrument for assisting us in becoming successful in life. We can maximize our potential and achieve our goals by using technology to interact with others, manage tasks, keep organized, and access information.

Make the most of your strengths.

Everyone possesses unique talents, abilities, and qualities that can be leveraged to further their success. Knowing and understanding our personal strengths and how to effectively utilize them will assist us in achieving our goals and dreams.

First and foremost, we must discover our personal strengths. We can better understand ourselves and what we are capable of by partaking in activities that bring out our abilities. For example, if you're a great communicator, use that skill to connect with others and form deep bonds. You may then leverage these ties to your advantage, whether it's by networking for a job or collaborating with others to achieve a common goal.

Furthermore, if you have a talent for math or science, use it to get a degree in that discipline; if technology inspires and encourages you, investigate that field. When you understand and use your talents, you gain confidence in your abilities. Whether you're solving a problem or starting a business, having faith in your abilities helps you to take calculated risks and succeed. You get the confidence needed to face the challenge, create goals, and accept responsibility for your efforts and results.

Leveraging your abilities can lead to self-fulfillment in addition to achievement. It gives you a sense of accomplishment when you use your abilities to achieve your goals. Knowing that you are doing something worthwhile that corresponds with your values and interests can lead to a deeper sense of fulfilment that is difficult to obtain.

Improve your emotional intelligence.

It is commonly understood that emotional intelligence (EI) is a crucial component in determining life success. According to studies, emotional intelligence accounts for up to 80% of a person's success in life. This means that if you want to be successful in both your personal and professional lives, you must cultivate your emotional intelligence.

Understanding your own emotions as well as the feelings of others and being able to use these emotions to your benefit in life is what emotional intelligence entails. Emotional intelligence entails self-awareness, or the ability to control one's own emotions, as well as empathy, or the ability to comprehend and relate to the feelings of others. People's emotional qualities and skills are critical for successful engagement with others.

Increasing your emotional intelligence can help you achieve more success in life. It can help you notice and control your own emotions more effectively if you have a greater sense of self-awareness. This allows you to better regulate your emotions and be less reactive to bad situations. Being emotionally knowledgeable will also help you better understand and control your stress, allowing you to deal with stressful situations more effectively.

Furthermore, it might assist you in developing relationships with others. Being emotionally knowledgeable can help you relate to people better by making you a better listener and less judgmental. Furthermore, emotional intelligence can help people gain trust and respect in their relationships with others.

Increasing emotional intelligence also aids in decision-making. Understanding and being aware of one's emotions might assist a person in slowing down their thought process and better weighing out a decision before diving in. People who are more aware of the effects of emotions can readily notice when they are anxious or nervous, which can make them better prepared to consider those sentiments before making a decision.

Finally, emotional intelligence can help people gain more control over their emotions in a variety of settings. Being emotionally intelligent implies you can better understand and plan for how your emotions influence your actions, as well as develop techniques to regulate them. This can lead to better performance in both personal and professional settings.

To summarize, emotional intelligence is a crucial aspect in obtaining life success. Emotional intelligence can improve self-awareness, help people construct better relationships, help people make more informed decisions, and give people more control over their emotions. Thus, emotional intelligence is required for success in any sector.

Exercise self-care.

Self-care is critical for long-term success. It enables you to stay focused, invigorated, and motivated while working towards your objectives. Self-care helps to maintain your mind and body healthy, which is required to meet life's obligations. Self-care is vital for building a strong foundation for a successful life. It includes everything from getting enough rest and relaxation to eating healthily, exercising regularly, making time for leisure activities, setting good boundaries, and more.

Making time for yourself and your health is essential for corporate employees. Adequate sleep can aid with cognitive processing and productivity, while regular exercise can help with stress, depression, and anxiety. To get the most out of self-care, it's critical to establish healthy behaviors that can be maintained regularly. Eating a well-balanced diet, taking frequent pauses during the day, and maintaining a consistent sleep schedule are all good strategies to practice self-care.

Having supportive relationships in your life, such as with family, friends, or a therapist, can also be beneficial. These interactions can help you stay focused and motivated by providing structure and support. Setting clear limits might also help you feel empowered to say "no" to things for which you do not have the time or energy. This can assist minimize burnout and keep you motivated to keep moving forward.

When pursuing academic or professional achievement, it is critical to ensure that you are also practicing self-care. Taking regular pauses, getting adequate sleep, eating good meals, and limiting your use of social media can all help you be more productive, creative, and focused. Hobbies and leisure activities can also assist relieve stress and re energize your brain.

Above all, remember that self-care does not have to be difficult or time-consuming. Small changes to your daily routine, such as stretching for a few minutes in the morning, meditating, or going for a walk, can help you stay not just physically healthy, but also psychologically and emotionally balanced.

Overall, self-care is critical for life success. Engaging in activities that encourage good behaviors, give relaxation, and create a feeling of balance on a regular basis will help you stay on track while you work towards your goals. You, too, can learn to practise self-care and be successful in life by persistently following behaviours that enhance mental, physical, and emotional well-being.

Maintain your organization.

One of the most important things you can do to attain success in life is to keep organized. This is due to the fact that an efficient organization can help you better manage your time and efforts, remain on top of your priorities, set attainable goals, and eventually lead to increased productivity and success.

Staying organized, for example, can help you make the most of your time by having a clear method for properly arranging chores. You can develop a daily to-do list that describes your daily goals and ensures nothing falls between the cracks. You may also plan out your day's responsibilities ahead of time and establish deadlines to hold yourself accountable. Staying organised allows you to make the most of each day while working towards your goals.

Organization can also assist you in setting attainable goals. It might be difficult to track and quantify success without a clear plan. However, by structuring your efforts and breaking down your larger goals into smaller objectives, you may concentrate on the specific tasks required for achievement. Staying organised allows you to track your triumphs and failures and make quick course corrections if something isn't working.

Additionally, structure can assist reduce stress and enhance focus. When everything is in order, it is simpler to prioritize duties and prevent the stress that comes from juggling many chores or forgetting something crucial. It also allows you to track your progress and celebrate tiny victories, which may be powerful motivators to keep going.

Finally, being organized allows you to be more productive. Organization allows you to streamline procedures, perform jobs more quickly, and prioritise tasks that bring the greatest value to your overall goals. This will pave the road for a prosperous future.

To summarize, remaining organized is essential for success in life. It assists you in organizing your time and efforts, setting attainable goals, reducing stress, and remaining productive. As a result, if you want to be successful, you must have a clear method for organizing and organizing your work.

Take the initiative.

Taking the initiative is a critical component of achieving success in life. It is the capacity to perceive an opportunity and act on it without relying on others to tell you what to do. It entails pushing yourself out of your comfort zone, making decisions, and taking chances.

With your passion and drive, having initiative allows you to stand out from the crowd. It demonstrates your ability to think beyond the confines of your current task and develop innovative solutions. It can be especially useful early in your career because it demonstrates to employers that you are capable of taking on more and more demanding duties.

Here are a few examples of how taking the initiative might help you succeed:

- Identifying problems and providing answers When you take the initiative to identify problems and present realistic and actionable solutions, it demonstrates that you are a strategic thinker who cares about the overall success of the company.
- Seeking new possibilities or projects If you are capable of identifying possible opportunities or projects, you can take the initiative and submit them to your company. This demonstrates initiative and resourcefulness, and it frequently leads to larger and better chances in the future.
- Taking up new challenges. Taking the initiative implies that you are eager to tackle new

problems and broaden your knowledge and skill set. Whether it's learning a new language or attending business classes, demonstrating your eagerness to learn shows employers that you're dedicated to self-improvement.

- Being proactive rather than reactive. You will be proactive rather than reactive if you take the initiative. Instead of waiting for tasks to come to you, you plan ahead of time and think of unique methods to tackle them. Being proactive demonstrates that you can solve problems and think on your feet.
- Adaptability. Recognising and accepting that conditions and the environment are continuously changing and adapting accordingly will help you successfully navigate new circumstances.

More opportunities will come your way if you take the initiative. It is an essential component of obtaining success since it demonstrates your ambition, resourcefulness, and resilience. Furthermore, it distinguishes you in a competitive employment market. So, if you want to be successful, take the initiative and wait for good things to come your way.

Change requires adaptation.

One of the most critical qualities to have in order to attain success in life is the ability to adapt to change. Most of us experience change on a regular basis, therefore it is critical that we learn how to manage it and use it to our benefit. We can make better judgments, make better use of resources, and generate new opportunities when we can predict, identify, and respond to changes in our environment.

One of the most important advantages of adapting to change in life is that it keeps us informed and involved in our goals. We can negotiate the sometimes unanticipated and uncomfortable facts of life by responding swiftly and properly to changes. We can also use the changes to our advantage, making it easier to reach our objectives.

For example, when the employment market changes, such as layoffs or new job vacancies, individuals who can react and capitalize on the changes are more likely to succeed. Those who refuse to change their ways are left in the dust. Change can also boost creativity and innovation. When we are confronted with a shift in our surroundings, we have the opportunity to think outside the box and devise fresh ideas that can help us develop our careers or personal goals. We can also use our creative energy to generate new chances or techniques that were previously unavailable.

When we welcome change and seek new solutions in our environment, we can also use it as an opportunity to learn and grow. By experimenting with novel approaches to issues and opportunities, we can improve our skills and knowledge, making us better equipped for the future.

Finally, learning to adapt to change allows us to enjoy the current moment and find joy in the process. With each new situation, we can try new things and broaden our horizons, helping us to be more present in the moment and enjoy life to the fullest.

Change, without a question, may be difficult and painful at times. However, if we take the time to learn and appreciate it, we may reap the many advantages of adaptation and use it to our advantage in life.

Develop new skills.

Learning new talents is vital for obtaining success in life. You can advance in both your personal and professional lives by taking on new tasks and responsibilities with new talents. You will be able to tackle any task that comes your way if you have a diverse skill set.

To begin, it is critical to prioritize mastering the fundamentals. Learning the fundamentals of reading, writing, math, and computer use can help you master more advanced courses in the future. Furthermore, these fundamental ideas are required for tackling increasingly sophisticated activities like programming or financial trading. They also serve as a foundation for more particular abilities like public speaking, photography, and computer programming.

As you advance, it may be beneficial to begin focusing on skills linked to your chosen professional path. It's critical for doctors, for example, to stay up to date on medical scientific advances. Attending seminars and webinars, as well as joining professional organizations in your sector, can help you achieve this. Engineers, too, must keep up with the latest technology and techniques.

Broadening your knowledge can also help you improve your credentials, which can help you advance in your work. You can begin by enrolling in courses that interest you and have possible job applications. A person interested in finance, for example, may profit from economics and investment classes. Furthermore, broadening your knowledge of a certain area might help you better grasp the employment market and the types of positions that may be accessible to you.

Strong interpersonal skills might also be advantageous. Understanding how to communicate successfully with your team, creating relationships with coworkers, and understanding workplace dynamics are all part of this. Working with various groups and creating an environment where everyone can succeed can be important to your success. Learning new talents can help you succeed in life. However, it is critical to remember that learning is a constant process that necessitates effort, patience, and attention. Once you've learned the fundamentals and are comfortable with your existing skill set, you should always push yourself to learn more.

Finding an inspirational mentor to help guide you through your journey will help you make the most of your efforts. Having a subject matter expert on your side will not only provide the essential information, but also invaluable advice that will help you stay focused during difficult times. You will be on your way to success if you take the time to constantly study and grow.

Improve your problem-solving skills.

Problem solving is an essential ability to have since it allows one to think critically and creatively about whatever issues they may face. It is a critical component of success because it prepares individuals to generate innovative ideas and traverse the ever-changing landscape of the twenty-first century. The ability to identify and understand an issue, generate viable answers, and come up with an effective solution is required for problem solving. Individuals should exercise the following stages to become an efficient issue solver:

- Identifying the problem: Look at the problem from a new angle and evaluate all of its components, such as the root cause and contributing causes, to acquire a better understanding of the problem you're attempting to address.
- Analyzing the problem entails thinking through the scenario, identifying problem areas, and weighing the advantages and drawbacks of prospective remedies.
- Brainstorming potential solutions: Think about how different ideas can help address the problem.
- Implementing a solution entails deciding on the best alternative and taking the necessary steps to make it a reality.

In addition to following these procedures, it is critical to be adaptable while issue solving. This includes being willing to make changes if a proposed solution does not work and being willing to compromise. It also entails having a growth mentality and being willing to take chances. Finally, problem-solving abilities are required for individuals to achieve their objectives and become successful.

A student, for example, who is having difficulty studying for an upcoming exam can use problem-solving skills to create a study plan that is suited to their specific needs. They can come up with several potential answers through brainstorming, such as generating task lists, setting realistic goals, breaking the subject down into manageable portions, or getting assistance from peers or instructors. The student can achieve their intended aim of passing the exam by applying a solution and taking action.

Similarly, a business owner might employ problem-solving abilities to create a strategy for increasing sales and profits. They can assess the present situation and find areas for improvement, develop potential sales techniques, and implement the best strategy for their organization. The business owner can achieve their goal of growing sales and money by using problem-solving skills.

Overall, problem-solving abilities are required for success in all areas of life. It is critical to be able to appraise a situation, produce potential answers, then put those solutions into action. It is also critical to maintain flexibility and a growth mentality. Individuals can achieve their goals and be successful if they have good problem-solving skills.

Stay result-oriented.

Staying results-oriented allows you to stay focused and get things done while also allowing you to track your progress. Here are some examples of how being results-oriented can help you succeed:

1. Set Goals: Setting specific goals might help you stay focused on the task at hand. Goals provide a framework for monitoring development and something to strive for. For example, if you want to get a 4.0 GPA in college, you can set

reasonable goals for each semester to help you get there.

2. Effective Time Management: Being results-oriented entails actively planning your day and controlling your time. To be organized and productive, it's critical to schedule chores ahead of time and use tools like calendars or to-do lists. Planning ahead of time can also help you anticipate potential problems and generate remedies before they occur.

3. Keep Track of Your success: Staying results-oriented entails keeping track of your success over time and making modifications as needed. Regularly monitoring your progress assists in identifying areas where improvements could be made or where additional development is required. Tracking sales and customer feedback over time, for example, might help you identify areas where additional resources or modifications could be needed to achieve success if you're attempting to build a business.

4. Take Action: Taking action is essential for remaining results-oriented. To assure growth and discover prospective opportunities and difficulties, you must take regular measures. To assess progress, for

example, if your aim is to become a better public speaker, you must take action by attending networking events and practise your talks.

Overall, remaining results-oriented can assist you in becoming successful in life. You may stay focused and motivated to attain your goals by actively assessing your progress and taking action when necessary. By concentrating on outcomes, you may utilise quantifiable goals to track your progress and take the required steps to ensure success.

Develop innovative approaches to increasing production.

There is no doubt that creativity is a valuable instrument for achieving personal success. A creative approach to problem solving is widely acknowledged to have numerous advantages, including greater productivity and innovation in both our personal and professional life. Cultivating innovative approaches to boost productivity is critical for everyone seeking success.

One of the primary advantages of using a creative approach to problem solving is that it allows us to break free from conventional thinking and develop novel solutions to problems. It allows us to look at a problem from a different angle and come up with new solutions. Furthermore, innovation has the capacity to produce more efficient and productive processes. A creative person, for example, can develop unique, outside-the-box ways to do jobs faster and with higher quality.

Furthermore, when establishing ways to boost productivity through creativity, it is critical to consider the "big picture," or how a creative solution to an issue might benefit not only in the near term but also in the long run. Furthermore, by understanding the interdependence of tasks, it is possible to demonstrate how creative solutions might save time and effort in the long term.

Finally, creative problem-solving is about determining the optimum answer for a given circumstance in order to optimize production and success. When attempting to boost productivity, it is critical for individuals to remain open-minded and explore all available possibilities in order to make the optimal decision for the current setting. Individuals must also keep an optimistic outlook and be willing to accept failure in order to learn and develop from the experience in order to get the most of this strategy.

Overall, it is obvious that creating innovative approaches to boost productivity is critical to success. Using this technique has the ability to open up new opportunities, expose us to fresh viewpoints, and result in better outputs that can assist our efforts. Anyone can improve their chances of success by actively embracing creativity and a willingness to explore alternatives.

Take frequent pauses.

It is common knowledge that taking regular breaks from work and other mental or physical activity can improve both productivity and general health. Taking regular pauses improves our focus, reduces stress, improves our physical health, and even improves our mental health. It is thus an essential component of achieving success in life, and here's why:

For starters, taking regular breaks allows us to stay focused. It provides us an opportunity to clear our minds, allowing us to return to our tasks refreshed. For example, we can take a 5-minute walk around the office or parking lot to get some fresh air. Furthermore, breaks allow us to refocus on our tasks and better prioritise our actions. Taking a few moments during the day to pause and reflect on our objectives can help us keep on track and inspired.

Second, taking breaks can help us relax. We allow ourselves to exit work mode when we take a break. This can help us relax and relieve stress in our minds and bodies. Furthermore, taking breaks allows us to free up our thoughts and ideas, allowing us to come up with new solutions to challenges we have been having difficulty tackling.

Finally, taking breaks can benefit our physical health. Sitting for long periods of time without getting up can strain our backs and necks, impair our posture, and make us more prone to developing diseases like diabetes. To fight this, get up and move around for at least 5 to 10 minutes every hour or so. This can also raise your heart rate, which leads to increased circulation throughout your body and better sleep. It can also enhance our mental health. Regular breaks can help lessen feelings of anxiety and sadness by allowing us to breathe and release some of the stress that we are carrying. Taking a few moments during the day to calm our brains can help build a sense of self-appreciation and keep our mental and emotional well-being in check.

In conclusion, taking regular breaks helps to improve our focus, reduce stress, improve our physical health, and even our mental health. It can assist us in remaining productive and motivated, thus assisting us in becoming more successful in life. So, don't be scared to take a break when necessary; it might just be what you need to move ahead.

Have faith in yourself and your ability.

The power of self-belief is a tremendously powerful instrument that may transform seemingly insurmountable goals into realities. While stepping outside of your comfort zone to attain your full potential can be scary, believing in your talents and having trust in the process can be the foundation for your success.

When you believe in yourself, you may take the measures necessary to make your aspirations a reality. Having the inner strength to persevere in the face of adversity lays a solid basis for resilience and achievement. You will have the confidence to take risks in life and attain greater success. Instead of feeling defeated by challenges or obstacles, you grow more capable of rising to them.

The story of **J.K. Rowling** is one illustration of how believing in yourself may help you achieve success in life. Rowling. She was a single mother struggling to make ends meet, and despite several rejections from book publishers, she remained optimistic about the possibilities of her novel. She continued to write and pitch her work until the Harry Potter series was formed. Rowling transformed an idea into a business behemoth and is now a well-known novelist.

<u>Bill Gates</u> is another case in point. Despite little resources, he worked relentlessly to build Microsoft into the global powerhouse it is today. He used his expertise and skills to self-motivate to overcome obstacles and make his ambition a reality. Many people questioned him, but he remained solid in his faith and belief in himself.

Believing in yourself and your abilities clarifies your goals and gives you the resolve to achieve them. It builds strength and resilience, preparing you to deal with any scenario in life. It opens the door to limitless possibilities and assists you in reaching greater heights of accomplishment. So, if you have faith in yourself and your ability, the possibilities are limitless.

Keep a positive attitude.

Maintaining a happy attitude is critical in deciding how well we do in many aspects of life, from profession to relationships to personal health. A positive attitude can help us stay motivated, keep on track, and achieve greater achievements in both our professional and personal life.

Maintaining a good attitude has an effect on our lives by assisting us in remaining motivated and interested in whatever we set out to do. When faced with difficulties, maintaining a positive attitude motivates us to seek answers and keeps us from giving up. It also helps us be productive through times of stress or burnout since it allows us to stay focused on the task at hand in order to reach our goals.

Positive attitudes can aid in the formation and maintenance of effective partnerships. We can build lasting connections based on trust and understanding if we adopt a more hopeful outlook on life. A cheerful attitude in conversations helps to build connections with others, which can lead to healthier interactions. A positive attitude towards individuals around us can help us adapt to new conditions more quickly since we are more likely to be receptive to new experiences and ideas.

Positivity has an effect on our physical wellbeing as well. When we think positively, our bodies release endorphins, which make us feel good. This happiness transfers into physical health as our immune systems strengthen and we are better able to deal with the stressors of daily life.

Finally, in order for a person to attain their greatest potential, they must maintain a positive mindset. We are more likely to take risks and embrace difficulties that will lead us to success if we have a positive view on life. It keeps our wits sharp and allows us to solve challenging situations more swiftly and strategically.

Conclusion

This book has presented the numerous lessons and guidance required to live a meaningful life in the twenty-first century. This book is a compendium of knowledge and methods for persons of all ages wishing to create something of themselves, ranging from practical tips on professional success and financial literacy to life hacks on organization and being up to date on current events and trends.

The capacity to notice possibilities, practice self-discipline, and balance work and play are all qualities that will aid in the creation of a successful and accomplished environment. The more that can be done to keep ahead of the curve in the modern world of work, the better. Setting and achieving goals, as well as having a solid support system, are all necessary for self-actualization and job success.

Organization and efficiency will also be important factors in achieving success in life and at business. Budgeting, time management, process optimisation, and carefully utilizing spare time are just a few of the numerous factors to consider for increased productivity. Make it a habit to create both online and offline networks, and make an ongoing effort to be educated and up to date on the latest technology.

A healthy balance of life's facets will assist you in prioritizing what is genuinely important. The greatest approach to ensure success is to learn how to stay focused and motivated while living a life that matches your values and objectives.

You don't have to be the smartest or wealthiest person to attain your objectives. Success and happiness are frequently found in the journey and the experiences along the way. Failure is a risk that comes with success and growth. Fortunately, even adversity may be used to learn, grow, and improve one's life skills.

At the end of the day, the individual determines success. It is possible to build the vision and habits that will mold a prosperous life and career using the life lessons provided in this book.